FEEL LIGHT

STRESS MANAGEMENT FOR LIFE

John Beckman

Copyright © 2012 John Beckman

Legal Disclaimer

CONTENTS

5 EFFECTIVE EXERCISES FOR MANAGING STRESS LEVELS

In today's fast-paced and busy world, stress is not an unfamiliar concept. Be it managing a home, school, or work, there is always some form of stress to occupy some aspect of one's life. And while there are some people who are able to deal with stress amazingly well, there are others who can't seem to cope with it. Succumbing to stress can imply health or emotional problems, which means that the person cannot function properly anymore.

Fortunately, there are a few DIY ways in which you can de-stress and try to relax a little bit. These are simple exercises that you can do from where you are to trigger a mellower, more relaxed vibe. The beauty of these exercises are they also keep you healthy to an extent apart from just helping you de-stress at that certain moment.

Here are 5 effective exercises to help you calm down when your stress levels are sky-high:

BREATHING TECHNIQUES

Sometimes, even simple breathing will do the trick for you. Have you ever experienced doing a public speaking engagement? If public speaking isn't your thing, have you noticed how your tummy goes into annoying butterflies, your hands go clammy, you feel the sudden urge to barf or pee, and your mouth is so incredibly dry? These are often signs of last-minute stress, which can affect your performance. All you have to do is breathe in and out slowly and deeply. Couple this with a glass of lukewarm water and you should slowly feel more relaxed and less frantic. For the breathing technique to work, you have to make sure that you are breathing in deeply and are exhaling slowly.

STRETCHING EXERCISES

Another way to manage stress is by doing stretching. Scientifically speaking, stretching helps reduce stress by promoting great blood circulation in your body. This makes sure that blood goes to the right parts of your body, keeping your energy levels up and your muscle tension down. Ever wondered why it always feels so good to have stretching exercises done on you after a relaxing massage? Stretching is a good way to make sure that everything is in the right place, making you feel more comfortable.

THE YOGA 3-PART BREATHING EXERCISE

Yoga is one of the most relaxing physical activities for men and women, and while you do work up a sweat, you feel more relaxed at the same time because of all the stretching. This yoga 3-part breathing exercise is called pranayama and can be accomplished in a few simple steps. The first is to lie on your back, close your eyes, and relax all the muscles in your body. Second, start observing the natural way in which you inhale and exhale. Release every other thought from your mind and focus on your breathing. Third, start inhaling through the nose very deeply. Make sure that your stomach expands with each inhale. Do this 5 times. On the 6th time, do it again, but fill up your belly more so that your rib cage expands.

AEROBIC EXERCISES

True to form, physical movement also helps you relax. Exercise activates endorphin, which is the "happy hormone", allowing you to be more comfortable and relaxed. This is why many people blow off steam by going to the gym for a rigorous training session. It keeps their mind off the subject of stress and the burning of calories also helps them feel more relaxed.

MEDITATION

Meditating leads you to a more peaceful state of mind, and stress, more than anything, has everything to do with state of mind. Once your mind is at ease, the rest of your body will follow.

VISUALIZATION

It is a universal fact that no person can claim to never have experienced a stressful situation before in his or her life. People will inevitably encounter stressful situations that often times require her or him to make life-changing decisions. Whether the source of stress is a dysfunctional family, a broken relationship, grades, or a work-related problem, a stressed-out person must learn to deal with burnout and the mood swings, or else he or she will succumb to it-- not good nor healthy.

It is often said that stress is a state of mind, and that you can only be stressed as much as you allow it to get to you – and this is certainly true. Often times, the one barrier to the problem's solution can be our way of dealing with stress. If we do not deal with it well and sulk in one corner of the room while waiting for the problem to solve it, stress is prolonged and may sometimes start affecting other people. Because stress is a state of mind, your mind is therefore is key to helping relieve the stress you are feeling.

Therefore, the solution to stress must be something that will directly calm the mind.

One of the more useful and effective techniques is visualization. Beyond the massages and the exercising, visualization directly targets the chemical source of stress—your brain and emotions—so that you feel calmer and ready to take on the problem. If you can get your mind to a more peaceful state, then the rest of your body will follow. It is usually when you start feeling or deciding something that the rest of your body follows suit to what your brain is saying.

How can you use visualization to ease stress? It's pretty simple. Think of what makes you happy, secure and peaceful. Now this may differ from person to person. Someone's peaceful picture may be gentle meadows and soft green grass, while others may envision it to be a room filled with classical music. Think of your own peaceful picture, and fill your mind with it whenever you are feeling the effects of stress, and this should eventually calm you down.

Another visualization technique would be to imagine an ideal end. Think of your end goal and how happy you would be if you were able to attain it. This should get you motivated to push on and stop stressing out.

No matter what type of visualization technique you use, as long as it works for you, learn to use it regularly in times of stress. You should know what can calm you or help you relax-- and knowing this, you should put it to good use whenever your mind and body call for it.

LAUGHTER, THE BEST MEDICINE: LET'S LAUGH AWAY THE STRESS

Another great breathing exercise is to combine deep breathing with a visualization technique. This simply means that you must visualize something positive while slowly and deeply breathing in and out to help enforce positive thinking. Think of something you would like to accomplish – possibly a life goal – or optionally, paint a peaceful picture in your head – for some, these may be scenes of nature, while for others, it may be certain people or types of music. Whatever your peaceful picture is, visualize it in your head and keep breathing in and out in a controlled manner. This helps re-energize and re-motivate you to move forward.

While everyone's ideal world is a lifestyle free of stress, this isn't the reality. People will inevitably encounter a form of stress, be it work, family or school-related, and some will often find it quite difficult to deal with.

There are many reasons behind this scenario. The first may be that the person doesn't really know how to stop and take a break when stress is overwhelming them. This is often the type of person who prefers to continue working late into the night without stopping, despite fatigue and a pounding headache. With stress, breaks are often needed so that your body and mind can rejuvenate and re-energize. Another reason is that the person is overwhelmed with too many problems to deal with the situation. There are certain types of people who easily break down at the first sign of too much stress. When he or she has got too much to handle, none of the problems get solved and the person tries to run away from it. Finally, the last reason may be that the person takes himself or herself too seriously. Everything is often infused with dramatic endings and emotional outbursts.

This last reason is one of the more popular reasons behind stress. Often times, even though we realize that we can only do what we can, we tend to be too hard on ourselves and still expect to be able to find the ideal solution to the problem when there is none. In this case, the best medicine for stress is laughter.

Now you may be wondering how laughter is a valid and legit relaxing technique in times of stress. There is simply something very uplifting and relaxing about laughing. You can take away the heaviness or burden of the situation by trying to find humor in it. While some people scoff at this technique as a way to escape and not face the situation, there are other times when laughter is greatly needed. Take, for instance, a situation where work has unexpectedly piled up with the same urgent deadlines. Now, a really emotional and stressed-out person may start crying, sulking, and staring at the paperwork without really doing anything. But a person who uses laughter to deal with it is able to just laugh it off, knowing that he or she will have to do it anyway. This lightens up the mood and the heavy feeling in his or her chest so that he or she is motivated to plow through the work.

While laughter is good in most stressful situations, a person must remember to use it wisely and in good time, as it may be offensive to other people or awkward in a social situation. However, the bottom line is that laughter is infectious and is very heartwarming. If you can laugh at yourself or find humor in a stressful situation, you are very lucky as you can use this as a way to de-stress and maybe even take a short break before plunging back in.

TOP 10 ANXIETY FIGHTING FOODS

Another great breathing exercise is to combine deep breathing with a visualization technique. This simply means that you must visualize something positive while slowly and deeply breathing in and out to help enforce positive thinking. Think of something you would like to accomplish – possibly a life goal – or optionally, paint a peaceful picture in your head – for some, these may be scenes of nature, while for others, it may be certain people or types of music. Whatever your peaceful picture is, visualize it in your head and keep breathing in and out in a controlled manner. This helps re-energize and re-motivate you to move forward.

Another great breathing exercise is to combine deep breathing with a visualization technique. This simply means that you must visualize something positive while slowly and deeply breathing in and out to help enforce positive thinking. Think of something you would like to accomplish – possibly a life goal – or optionally, paint a peaceful picture in your head – for some, these may be scenes of nature, while for others, it may be certain people or types of music. Whatever your peaceful picture is, visualize it in your head and keep breathing in and out in a controlled manner. This helps re-energize and re-motivate you to move forward.

While the usual ways of dealing with stress include breathing exercises and physical activity, most people do not know that there are actually foods that help reduce stress and make you feel calmer and more relaxed. Knowing what types of food to take when

You're feeling a little bit or severely stressed will help you cope with it better, and people who have an aversion to exercise can find that the right type of food can be a good alternative. Here is a list of the top ten foods to take for stress relief.

1.   BLUEBERRIES

Blueberries have huge amounts of Vitamin C, which is the vitamin known for aiding the body in its fight against stress. In addition, blueberries have a lot of fiber, and you should know that this helps keep your sugar levels in check. When your sugar levels change constantly, this can trigger stress.

2.   WATER

If you have ever experienced a dry mouth and throat before a major event in your life, water is your best solution to stress. Not only will it help you breathe better, it will also hydrate your body so that it does not grow weak and faint.

3.   LOW FAT OR SKIM MILK

With lots of calcium and B vitamins, low fat or skim milk helps keep your nerves in check. Nerves are one of the major causes of stress, especially when they tell the person to feel emotionally distressed. Also, with a good amount of protein, it helps keep your blood sugar at a stable level.

4.   SWEET POTATO

Sweet potatoes are a great source of good sweetness. People often crave for something sweet when they are stressed, and these are a great alternative to your chocolate bars and cookies.

5. ORANGES

Because these are also chock full of Vitamin C, they will help relieve stress.

6. SOY

Soy (whether as milk or tofu) has lots of B vitamins, protein, magnesium and calcium, and helps you feel calm and relaxed in the midst of a stressful situation.

7. BROWN RICE

A type of whole grain, brown rice is great for relieving stress as this contains plenty of vitamin B and fiber.

8. TURKEY

Turkey meat contains a very special acid called L-Tryptophan, which aids the reduction of stress by inducing the brain to feel good. Another alternative you can try is chicken (but don't fry it or it will lose its effect).

9. GREEN VEGETABLES

These help calm your nerves as they contain the necessary vitamins that have a calming effect on your system.

10. DRIED APRICOTS

Dried apricots are amazingly great-tasting and contain a lot of magnesium, which is known to relieve stress. Magnesium is also known to help relax muscles, and dried apricots also contain a lot of Vitamin C and fiber.

HEAL YOURSELF WITH WORDS – HOW DIARY KEEPING CAN MINIMIZE STRESS

Healing yourself with words is exactly what it says - using the written word to help you to identify what it is that is causing you to feel stressed or anxious. By that I mean you should get yourself a diary or even a notebook and begin to record your feelings.

If you feel stressed, write it down and also note the time of day and what it was that caused you to feel that way. Obviously, you can't whip out your diary every ten minutes if you are having a particularly stressful day. So try and get out your diary every hour or so and record your feelings during the past hour.

Maybe use a scale of 1 to 10 to determine the amount of stress that you have felt in the previous hour. Record the event that caused you to feel that way and what it was about that event that made you feel stressed and how you dealt with the situation. Once you have written the stressful incident down, put the diary away and forget about that incident. Then repeat the process an hour later. Don't spend time looking back at the previous entries in your diary; leave that until you have at least ten days or so of entries.

After you have kept a 'stress diary' for a few weeks, you should sit down and review it. What situations made you feel most stressed? What did you do about it? Could you have handled it differently? Was there a particular time of day that had more stressful events? etc. You may find that there is a pattern to the stress that you feel - maybe you are easily stressed just after lunch or midafternoon. If that is the case, you can take steps to avoid the situations that cause you the most stress.

If your job is very stressful and you tend to be more stressed at work, try and change your hours and tasks around so that you will not have to do important tasks when you are most likely to feel stress. Try doing the most important tasks as early in the day as you can. Then take a few minutes to record in your diary how good it feels to know that a task has been completed successfully.

If you have had a stress free day, write that in your diary – in big bold writing. Doesn't that feel good? Keeping a diary, even for just a few weeks, will help you identify any situations or events that make you feel bad or stressed. You will be surprised at how good it will feel once you know what is causing you to feel stressed and you can decided how to handle that particular situation in the future.

So, give it a try for a few weeks and see if you can identify your stress triggers by using the power of the written word – your written word.

HOW CRYING CAN BE A NATURAL STRESS RELIEVER

How many times in your life have you been told not to cry? When you were a child, your parents would probably have told you 'not to be a cry baby'. But crying is a natural function of the body and is part of our natural way to relieve emotional pressure. Having a good weep is very therapeutic and studies have proven that it is good for you.

If you continue hold back the tears that your body needs to shed, you will begin to feel worse. Crying is the mechanism that our bodies use for the natural release of tension and stress. Researchers have also discovered that emotional stress can cause a buildup of chemicals that can be dispersed through the tears, so a good weep will usually release tension and make you feel much better. So never deny yourself a good cry!

There are times when you cry at a wedding, when you feel proud or you could even laugh until you cry. It is deemed reasonable to cry on these occasions. So why would shedding a few tears when you are unhappy, feeling stressed or when you are depressed not be acceptable?

Once the tears have helped to flushed away the buildup of chemicals that accumulate during stressful times; the tension and stress would be relieved, allowing our body to relax. So you can now see that the body's way of ridding itself of the buildup of these chemicals is by releasing tears through crying.

Did you know that over 87% of women have said that they feel much better after a good cry? The sad thing about our society is the fact that men generally feel that it is not 'manly' to cry. But in today's stressful world, crying would be a great stress reliever for men as well as women.

Give it a try. If you find yourself miserable, stressed or depressed, go to a private place where you can have a good weep. You could just let the tears roll down your cheeks or you could have a great, gut wrenching sobbing cry - whatever works for you. Afterwards you will feel much better. You may want to try this at a time when you don't have to see anyone for a while afterwards to give you time to wash your face and apply cold water to your puffy eyes. Crying is a natural stress reliever and you will feel calmer, more relaxed and it will even help to concentrate the mind.

So, the next time that you feel tearful when you have had a particularly stressful day, don't try and hold it in – allow yourself the luxury of a good cry and see how quickly you begin to feel better.

HOW TO NATURALLY RELIEVE STRESS WITH AROMATHERAPY

There are an increasing number of people, both men and women from all walks of life who suffer from stress. If you are one of these, don't worry, there are a number of ways to overcome this problem. You could resort to chemical treatments from your doctor or you could investigate the numerous alternative therapies that are available.

One of the most popular alternative therapies to help relieve stress is Aromatherapy.

Throughout history, aromas have been used for their ability to influence the state of mind. The use of incense in religion is an example of this. Studies have shown that there are two olfactory (used in smelling) nerves that run to the part of the brain that deals with memory and emotion; this is called the limbic system. This means that the aromas can evoke an immediate reaction within the brain.

The reduction of stress by aromatherapy is extremely effective; everyone loves a pleasant aroma and it has been proven that it can have a calming effect and lift the mood. Think about it; don't you feel good when you smell fresh coffee or honeysuckle in the hedgerows or even the smell of fresh baked bread when you walk past a bakery? What about smells that remind you of something nice that happened to you; for instance, the smell of a particular flower that was in your wedding bouquet or the smell of a tiny baby after they have been bathed.

So, aromatherapy for stress reduction works by introducing a calming state of mind using essential oils that are extracted from plants. The pleasant aroma of the essential oils sends a message to the feel good area of the brain (limbic system) which is why aromatherapy is very effective in helping with stress and emotional problems.

There lots of ways to use aromatherapy to reduce stress, including massage, oil burners, aromatherapy candles, a few drops of oil in your bath and even on bed linen.

There are several essential oils that are beneficial to anyone who is experiencing stress. Lavender is widely used along with chamomile (German or Roman) to help relax a stressed out body. Other useful oils for stress relief are Bergamot, Patchouli, Geranium, Citrus oils and Sandalwood.

If you are using aromatherapy oils for a massage, make sure that you add just a few drops of your chosen essential oil to a carrier oils like Almond oil. What could be better after a stressful day that having a relaxing aromatherapy massage?

If you don't have a partner to give you a relaxing massage and don't want to go to a beauty salon, try blending one or two of your favorite oils in an oil burner, light it then turn down the lights, put on some relaxing music and just sit quietly in a comfortable chair. The stresses of the day will just melt away.

So, if you find that you are suffering from stress, before dashing off to your doctor for prescription drugs, try some form of aromatherapy – you may find that you will feel much better in no time at all.

YOU ARE WHAT YOU THINK – HOW TO ELIMINATE STRESS AND ANXIETY WITH POSITIVE THINKING

With today's hectic lifestyle, more and more people are beginning to feel the effects of stress and anxiety. For a lot of people this can make day to day living a constant and never ending battle, but it need not be so. There is no need to rush off to the doctor for prescription drugs. The solution is within yourself.

A very wise man, Ralph Waldo Emerson once said "A man is what he thinks about all day long". So, using that analogy, if you continue to think that you cannot do something or that your life will never get better, then that is exactly what will happen. If you spend all day worrying about that which you cannot change, nothing will be achieved except that you will continue to feel bad.

In order to begin to eliminate the stress, worry and anxiety from your life, you need to change your way of thinking. Remove the words can't, won't, don't from your vocabulary. In fact, you should remove all negative words. If your head is full of thoughts like "I can't possibly do this" or "I don't know which way to turn" or even " they won't like me", you will not be able to find a solution to help you to eliminate the stress and anxiety from your life because you are constantly telling yourself that you 'can't or 'don't.

Begin each day by telling yourself that 'today will be a wonderful day' and believe it. Then, if you find yourself getting into a downward spiral of stress, remind yourself what you told yourself that morning.

As you go through the day, if you find yourself feeling any stress or anxiety, notice what type of thoughts you are having. There will, undoubtedly, be negative thoughts. Try consciously thinking to yourself "my day is going to get better" or "I can change the way I feel about ..." – then think about all the good things that are going to happen as a result of you not worrying. For instance, you will feel good, you will feel happier now that you know things are getting better and as a result of all that good, positive feeling, you will even look better. A calm, happy person looks so much better than someone who is showing a worried frown.

Be positive about every aspect of your life by remembering that there is nothing that you cannot do. Everything will always work out for you when you continually remind yourself of this. Each night when you get into bed, spend a few minutes remembering the good things about your day, give no attention to anything negative that happened but dwell on the positive. This practice will help you to focus on the positive in your life and allow your sleep to be uncluttered by negative feelings.

Everyone experiences stress and anxiety from time to time but it is how you deal with it that can make all the difference. Be positive and tell yourself regularly that your life is wonderful – and believe it!

DUMP YOUR STRESS BY EXPRESSING YOUR FEELINGS

Everyone suffers from stress at some point during their lives. A busy lifestyle, working more and more, financial or relationship problems can all leave little or no time to rest and relax and stress can become overwhelming if you don't take steps to unwind.

Stress can be a killer if not checked early. Heart problems could perhaps be the worst of a long list of ailments that can arise from too much stress, so how can one relieve stress?

There are a number of ways that people can rid themselves of stress and get back on the rails of living a healthy, stress free life, but first we must find out how we get stressed.

POTENTIAL CAUSES OF STRESS

1. Many people work too hard these days. A difficult job, tight deadlines or one that requires lots of working hours or taking work home with you can bring on stress as you're not allowing enough time to ease the pressure.

2. Financial problems can induce stress. With credit cards and loans available everywhere it's easy to get into a bind with constant pressures about affording repayments each week mounting.

3. Too much responsibility squeezed into each day can also become overwhelming. Dealing with family, work, relationships, household duties, social activities and more in each day can mean you end up feeling as though you're constantly under pressure.

These suggestions are only the tip of a very large iceberg when it comes to figuring out the potential causes of stress. However, no matter what the causes of your own stress might be, there are some ways you can help alleviate the pressure.

GET IT OFF YOUR CHEST

Talking to someone about the stress you are under can have a valuable impact on reducing stress and is an excellent stress management tool. Don't feel as if you are burdening the person or people you talk to as they have probably gone through some form of stress at some time during their lives and will be able to help you reduce the levels of stress you are under.

Managing stress can greatly reduce the risk of heart disease and heart attacks. Being stressed can result in high blood pressure and stomach problems, headaches and migraines, even a loss of your sexual appetite.

Stress relief is important if you want to lead a healthy lifestyle, and one of the ways of beating stress is by expressing your feelings. If you have a loved one then why not talk things over with them. A problem shared is a problem halved the saying goes and it is indeed true.

If you find it difficult to talk with loved ones or close family members, then a stress relief course can be a major benefit to you. Courses can involve you sitting in a group and talking about the problems you have and the level of stress you are under, all under the watchful eye of someone who is a professional in helping you to reduce your stress.

Another option you have open to you is to express your feelings when it comes to your employer's demands upon you in the work place. Be sure you're offering your opinion in a constructive and polite manner to point out your perspective in a rational way and your employer will be more understanding of your workload.

There are lots of ways you can adopt to reduce stress and expressing your feelings regarding a situation that you feel is overwhelming can really help you on your way to stress management.

EPSOM SALT – STRESS RELIEF'S BEST KEPT SECRET

If you're looking for an effective, simple way to enjoy a little stress relief, have you thought about Epsom salt?

There are many good uses for Epsom salts, but soaking in a hot bath with a couple of cups of Epsom salt added could be the number one way to quickly reduce the impact of stress on your body and leave you feeling relaxed and relieved.

We all experience periods of stress, but there are many different underlying causes for the stress we feel. Whether you feel pressured by work or by aches and pains plaguing you throughout each day, there is a way to get some relief.

EPSOM SALTS FOR STRESS RELIEF

The primary ingredient in Epsom salt is magnesium

sulfate, which is known to act as a mild sedative on the nervous system. Our bodies also need some magnesium, so absorbing a little through your skin can reduce inflammation.

Epsom salt also helps to reduce swelling and relaxes your muscles, so if you've had a difficult day and need to soothe an aching back or stiff joints, then a long hot bath with Epsom salts could be exactly what you need.

DETOXIFY

Epsom salt also has the ability to draw toxins out of your body, which can make you feel refreshed and take away that lethargic feeling. Many of us suffer from the effects of processed foods, chemicals, additives, preservatives, alcohol and other toxins that can accumulate in your body.

Soaking in a bath with some Epsom salt included can help draw out those toxins and improve your overall well-being.

FANCY FEET

If you've been on your feet all day, create a soothing foot bath with some Epsom salts. Magnesium sulfate can increase ionic strength, which can help prevent that 'prune' effect of soaking your feet even while it's relaxing the muscles, reducing swelling and soothing the skin.

BEAUTY SECRETS

Using Epsom salts can also have a great effect on your appearance too, as they have natural exfoliating properties. Exfoliation is excellent for removing dead skin cells and leaving fresh, healthy cells showing in their place.

You can also use Epsom salt to remove any excess oil or stubborn styling products from your hair to give it a healthy, full appearance. Your hair will feel cleaner and healthier than it's ever been before.

Smooth skin and healthy hair can give you a glowing, radiant appearance and as most women know, when you look good, you tend to feel good too.

Many people feel enormous amounts of stress when they struggle with acne or skin problems like eczema or dermatitis. It's possible to use Epsom salt in a poultice form to clear up many skin abrasions or blemishes.

The active ingredient in Epsom salt can act to dehydrate the inflamed areas beneath acne blemishes. You can add it to water to make a paste and apply it directly to your face to remove blackheads and pimples.

No matter what's causing your stress, it's possible to find stress relief by spending a little time soaking in a hot bath with some Epsom salts.

HOW TOUCH DEPRIVATION CAN AGGRAVATE STRESS

The average person is under an extreme amount of stress. Whether it's work, school, personal problems, or a combination of all of the above; we're all looking for ways to lessen that stress so that we can better enjoy our lives. It turns out it the thing that can relieve our stress is closer than we think.

Years ago scientists conducted a study on rhesus monkeys. They put a baby monkey in a cage with a surrogate mother. Of course this mother was just a stick with terry cloth over it. The baby monkey didn't know any better. It thought it was its mother and it hung on tight to it. That stick became its mother. Scientists then took another baby monkey and put it in a cage with another terry cloth surrogate mother; this one with a nipple attached that provided milk. These scientists found that the monkey who was able to enjoy the touch of its mother was happier than the monkey whose mother provided food and sustenance.

TECHNOLOGY

Believe it or not, most of us suffer from touch deprivation on a daily basis. With advances in technology, such as the iPhone, the Blackberry and even the personal computer, we're becoming more separated from one another on a daily basis. So essentially we're suffering from this touch deprivation, this lack of closeness from our fellow human beings, and it's making our lives extremely hard to live.

The average person still has family problems, work problems, and almost everyone has money problems. This has remained consistent throughout history. Yet our stress levels seem harsher today than any other time in history. Why is that? If scientists are correct, we can blame touch deprivation.

It's funny that we consider technology as bringing us closer together as a society. We can IM and email and chat and we consider that bringing us closer to one another. That's just not the case, however. An IM will never trump physical touch. An email will never equal a one on one with another person and typing away in a chat room will never be the same as sitting down with someone and having a discussion about life, or whatever you may talk about.

The fact is that touch deprivation is very real and it can exacerbate stress. That's not to say we need to do away with technology; it's only to say we need to spend an equal amount of time with actual human beings, touching and feeling and talking one on one, than we do chatting and IMing and emailing.

If people want to be happier, and feel lower amounts of stress, they need to consider the sense of touch and how important it is to the human emotion and the human spirit. We're all in this life together and we have an intrinsic need and desire to be touched. Not just sexually but in a friendly manner as well. It's imperative that we strive to avoid touch deprivation, and it's extremely necessary if we wish to do away with all the stress that's making our lives increasingly harder to endure.

HOW YOUR FACIAL EXPRESSIONS CAN DETERMINE YOUR MOODS

Our facial expressions have a lot of impact on our daily lives. They are one way we communicate with others. They have a lot to do with how we perceive others, how others perceive us and how we see ourselves.

In fact, even though we can't see ourselves most of the time, our facial expressions have the power to affect our moods. There are multiple reasons for this and all of them can affect how you feel throughout the day. It has been shown that relaxed people and those who smile a lot are normally happier and have fewer worries. People who are very tense and frown a lot have more stress to deal with.

Some people will make this a "chicken or the egg" argument. Does a person's life affect their expressions, or the other way around? The answer is definitely both. This is why using your own expressions to master your mood is such a powerful tool.

One reason why facial expressions have so much impact is because of what they do to the muscles of your face. Smiling relaxes a lot of the muscles and stretches others. This feels good. One of the best things you can do to put yourself in a better mood is to smile even if you don't feel like it. It doesn't have to be a big smile; just a little smile accompanied by a deep breath can change how you feel. Everything relaxes and you start feeling a little better right away. This may take some practice but it's been proven that it works.

If you are always frowning, you are literally scrunching up the muscles in your face. This causes a lot of tension in the face and this tension can spread to the neck and shoulders very easily. Nothing will improve if you keep frowning all the time. The tension will just multiply and put you in a bad mood. Coaxing yourself into relaxing is the best thing you can do to stop this vicious cycle.

Learning this ability is also important for your interactions with other people. Nobody really enjoys being around someone who always looks angry or upset. Even if it isn't a thought they realize they are having, they are worried that negativity will somehow rub off on them. This is a particular problem in business.

Most people have met a business owner or manager who has an angry or sour look on their face all the time. It is difficult to ever find out if that person is actually friendly or good at business because nobody wants to talk to them. Whether you are in business for yourself or you work for someone else, an unpleasant expression can lose you business and even get you passed over for promotions. This will only lead to more stress.

Having relaxed, pleasant facial expressions can do a lot for your career. Clients are more likely to choose to work with a cheerful business owner and bosses are more likely to promote happy employees.

The same principle is often true in relationships. When you smile at another person, they often smile right back at you. See what happens when you scowl at your partner instead of offering a smile.

As you can see, your facial expressions have a huge

impact on your mood, both directly and indirectly. By training yourself to have a relaxed, cheerful expression, you will improve how you feel and the way your life runs.

MANAGE STRESS WITH EFFECTIVE TIME MANAGEMENT

How many times have you felt as though you were trying to squeeze too much into each day? A big cause of stress for many people is the overwhelming feeling that there's too much to do and not enough time in which to get it done.

What many of these people don't understand is that they may not be making the best use of their time. If you knew you could get more accomplished through your day, yet take less time doing it, would that ease some of the pressure you put on yourself?

It's amazing how much you can get done when you put some simple time management tactics to work for you.

PRIORITIZE

Do you often find yourself working on tasks at work or at home that aren't really achieving the more important things you should be doing first? Many people spend time in damage control at work, answering phones, and doing any number of little chores that detract from the bigger tasks.

Create a priority list of things you need to get done through your day and work through them one at a time. Those emails can wait. Keep your phone calls short and sweet. Complete the important things and move less serious matters lower down the list to be completed when you have more time.

TIME WASTERS

How much time do you currently spend answering emails or checking social networking sites like FaceBook or MySpace? While these platforms can be great ways to keep up with friends and family, they are also huge time wasters capable of eating up hours of productive time during your day.

Limit the time you spend on these time wasters or

perhaps allocate a specific amount of time at the end of your day to work through these things.

TIME THIEVES

We all have time thieves in our lives who take up more time than you realize. Friends call to chat. Family drops in to visit. The short conversation turns into a couple of hours out of your day.

While you might feel social and relaxed while the time thief is there, as soon as they leave, the pressure of all those things you didn't get done comes crumbling down around your shoulders.

You may find that you can still get the same amount of social interaction and time to relax in a slightly shorter visit. This leaves you with more time left over to get things done and less stress on your plate.

PROCRASTINATION

Many people have learned to associate procrastination

with putting off the things they don't really want to do right now. Everything else seems more appealing and those tasks that you know should be done first get left longer and longer. This can mean you sub-consciously end up wasting a lot of time doing other things and creating a lot of stress.

Procrastination often stems from a dislike of the task at hand, however you can learn to break the procrastination cycle by re-adjusting your mindset a little. No matter how boring or arduous the task might be, understand that once it's done, you're free to do more enjoyable things.

SIMPLIFY

Time management doesn't necessarily need to be about squeezing more into each day. It can also mean learning to accept less tasks to complete each day too. After all, if you know you only have a few important tasks to get done today, you can work to get them done quickly and have the rest of the day doing things you enjoy more.

Learn to say no when people continue to put too much

pressure on the amount of time you have. Delegate some of your tasks to other people in the household or other colleagues at work.

Effective time management is about striking a balance between the tasks you need to get done as a priority and remembering not to heap too much onto your plate at the same time. Work on some basic time management tactics and you'll find you're more productive and less stressed.